The Amazing
Itty Bitty

Little Black Book of
Sales

15 Critical Steps to Power Selling
Unlock Your Earning Potential

Anthony Camacho

Published by Itty Bitty Publishing
A subsidiary of S&P Productions, Inc.
Copyright © 2015 Anthony Camacho

Printed in the United States of America

Itty Bitty Publishing
311 Main Street, Suite E
El Segundo, CA 90245
(310) 640-8885

ISBN: 978-1-931191-49-4

*I want to thank my Itty Bitty Ferry Godmothers –
Suzy Prudden for positively influencing me on the
idea that I could write an Itty Bitty Book and
Joan Meijer for all her guidance and wisdom
toward making it happen. This was the most fun
and amazing business project I have ever done in
my life. Thank you again to my Itty Bitty Ferry
Godmothers, Petie and Suzy.*

Table of Contents

Introduction

Having a strong selling ability is the 21st century's survival skill-set, equivalent to being a hunter back in the days of the hunter-gatherers.

In order to survive since the beginnings of civilization, you needed to know how to hunt. If you didn't hunt, you didn't eat. Excuses were not an option. Blaming didn't work. There were no salaries, there was no government assistance – you went out there with your two bare hands and made it happen. Survival depended on your hunting ability.

In the present economy, as manufacturing disappears, businesses fail and jobs are lost, sales becomes the new hunter skill in today's market. As you develop your selling skills, you will become invaluable to your company and family.

Having a positive – can do – attitude plus having a skilled selling ability puts you in high demand. This combination gives you job security, helps you get out of debt, allows you to set your own income goals and can give you a powerful lifestyle.

If you are a skilled sales person, you can survive any economic downturn. Selling is the most vital element in any business. Being a skilled sales professional keeps you in demand.

It doesn't matter how good your product or business is – if you don't know how to sell it, it won't make much difference.

Step 1

Mindset

Mindset is the most important element in achieving results, particularly in sales. It sets the tone for your life. It sets the tone for your day and it sets the tone for your sales. The mind will manifest whatever you tell it to in the physical world.

1. The first step in setting your mindset starts with belief in yourself,as well as believing in your product and your services.
2. By creating daily power affirmations and eliminating thoughts of weakness and negativity, you turn yourself into an unstoppable, powerful, super salesperson.
3. Become aware of the negative thoughts and emotions that hold you back; fear, worry, doubt, frustration, or feeling overwhelmed.
4. Create three words to oppose each of those thoughts or emotions.
5. Create a mantra and a positive affirmation out of those three power words.
6. Speak the affirmations aloud every morning.
7. Fill the energy of the negative emotion with the power of the positive affirmation.

Select Three Words That Work Against Negative Beliefs

- Worry (confident, prepared, courageous)
- Fear (brave, tenacious, unstoppable)
- Doubt (belief, bold, heroic)
- Overwhelmed (organized, steadfast, focused)
- Frustrated (calm, peaceful, resourceful)

If those words resonate with you, use them; if they don't, find words of your own that do.

Create a Positive Affirmation Using Those Three Words

- I am a confident, prepared and courageous salesman.
- Every day I find an unstoppable well of bravery and tenaciousness growing within me.
- My sales success is supported by my bold and heroic beliefs in myself.
- Each day I dedicate more of my time and energy to focusing on being organized, steadfast and focused on my sales success.
- Each morning I take time to center myself as a calm, peaceful and resourceful sales professional.

Choose an affirmation and focus on it. By consciously focusing on the affirmation, you leave no room for your old negative beliefs to impact on your abilities to achieve what you want.

Step 2

Visualization

You have to see it in your mind's eye first before you can accomplish or attain it.

1. Olympic gold medalists use visualization to win the gold.
2. Professional athletes use visualization in tournaments and competitions all over the world to be champions.
3. CEOs utilize visualization to build a successful company.

How Visualization Applies to You

- Visualize your idea of winning the gold.
- Visualize your full potential.
- Visualize being stretched beyond your comfort zone.
- Visualize the feeling of success.
- Visualize what type of person you need to be to attain that success.
- Visualize the people around you in that successful moment.
- Visualize the smile of your happy customer.
- Visualize the closing of the deal.
- Visualize the customer wanting the product.
- Visualize the customer needing the product.
- Visualize the customer using the product.
- Visualize the Win.
- Visualize how you're going to celebrate.

Step 3

Eliminate Self-Sabotage

Remove the negative habits that sales professionals use to sabotage their success and growth.

1. The blame game. Allowing yourself to become a victim to a person, place or thing.
2. Repeatedly saying:
   a. It's too hard to cold call.
   b. I'll never be able to get in front of Mr. CEO.
   c. The economy is too tough.
   d. The competition is too tough.
   e. They've been using my competitor forever.
3. Giving up.
   a. Not giving 100% to the customer.
   b. Not giving 100% to the process and procedures you represent.
   c. Not giving 100% to yourself.
4. Lack of Motivation.
   a. Working without true purpose.
   b. Working without true intention.
5. The "I know that" syndrome. Not paying attention and listening to the customer, which results in:
   a. First to lose sales.
   b. First to lose clients.
   c. First to lose revenue.
   d. First to complain.
   e. First to get laid off.

That which does not grow dies.

When you catch yourself expressing negative beliefs, perform this little exercise.

- "It's too hard to cold call." Say to yourself, "Cancel that thought." Replace it with the thought, "My cold calling becomes easier and more successful every day."
- "I'll never be able to get in front of Mr. CEO." Say to yourself, "Doors to Mr. CEO seem to open by magic. All I have to do is show up."
- "The economy is too tough." Say to yourself, "I make sales easily and effortlessly, even in a tough economy."
- "The competition is too tough." Say to yourself, "I am my competition's greatest and best competitor. I make sales where they can't."
- "They've been using my competitor forever." Say to yourself, "It is now time to show my new customer why I provide a better solution for their needs than my competition does."

Step 4

Return on Investment

There are only so many hours and only so much energy in a day. It is vital to eliminate thoughts, actions and behaviors that result in a negative Return on Investment (ROI).

1. Examples of negative ROI include:
    a. Coming to work unprepared gives you a negative ROI in terms of results.
    b. Thoughts of comparing what you didn't get with what someone else got wastes time and results in a negative ROI.
    c. Expressing anger and frustration provide a negative ROI.
    d. Failing to take control or being responsible for your time has a negative result.
    e. Worrying about rejection results in a negative ROI.
    f. Preconceived notions result in a negative ROI. The biggest of these notions is, "The customer can't afford it."
2. Sometimes sales professionals shy away and hide in some of these negative ROI actions because they're too afraid of the work and the dedication it's going to take to create sales.
3. We have to be careful to remain focused on the end result, which is to create more sales.

Return on Investment

- Internal
  - Have a daily purpose.
  - Create a daily intention.
- Performance
  - Know how much money you need to make every day.
  - Know how much money you need to make every month.
  - Identify money-making activities.
  - Maximize money-making activities.
  - Create benchmarks for each money-making activity.
    - A benchmark could be – make 20 follow-up calls.
    - A second benchmark could be – make 10 appointments.
    - A third could be – send out 25 emails.
    - A fourth could be – utilize social media, i.e. Facebook, etc.

Step 5

To Get Great Results
Be Creative and Resourceful

Take on 100% ownership and responsibility for both your action and your inaction.

1. Use the power of other people's successes and mistakes.
   a. Surround yourself with people who already have the result you want.
   b. Find mentors – people in the same industry as you are – and befriend them, ask them questions.
   c. Allow yourself to be mentored. Allow yourself to be coachable. Become a sponge to learning.
   d. Successful people are flattered by these questions.
2. Think outside of the box because there is no box. Just because certain things have been done one way doesn't mean they can't be done another way to get the same or better results.
3. Become a solution-based thinker. Write down every thought you have about how to create solutions and try them out. See if they work to get the results you want.
4. Be innovative. Have an innovative process. Talk to other people about your solution lists. Particularly talk to your mentors and other successful people in your field about your ideas.

Some Creative Resourceful Ideas

First, when you are going after the solution, you have to make the internal commitment to this kind of mentality. Decide to engage in solution-based thinking. Decide not to be swayed by anything else.

- Have a multi-dimensional view of solutions. Look at your solutions from every angle.
    - Angles include:
        - Being a user
        - Being the customer's end user
        - Experiencing successes and failures
- Become fixated on why a solution will work as opposed to why it won't work.
- Put your passion behind the solution.
- Put your drive behind the results.
- Put your energy into making the sale a positive, powerful experience.
- Good sales come out of the attraction of positive excitement.

Step 6

The Secrets of In-Person Cold Calling

I have made millions of dollars worth of sales from in-person cold calling. Cold calling is not limited to picking up the phone or sending an email. The secret to in-person cold calling is to go out and meet people. I believe the best sale comes from looking a customer in the eye.

1. Let people know that you are in existence in the market place.
2. Create friendships.
3. Create connections.
4. This is an opportunity to brand.
5. Letting people know who you are, what you do, and letting them know that they have choices.
6. Letting them know that you are another option for their business.
7. I would rather meet someone before I sell to them. In the same way I would rather meet someone in person before I date her online. Call me old fashioned…
8. There is nothing more powerful than the human experience.
9. There is nothing more exciting than the engagement of toe-to-toe conversation or sales.
10. For those who are introverts, this is going to help you change your relationship to cold calling. Even introverts have friends. Make this work for you the way you make friends.

The Secrets to In-Person Cold Calling

- It all starts with desired clients.
- Geographically map out where they work.
- If you are looking at several prospects, place your calls within a certain radius to save time.
- Plan on spending the whole day in that area.
- Have your business cards ready and start walking in some doors.
- The main objective on these cold visits is just to introduce yourself.
- Find out – by asking –who the decision maker is if you don't already know.
- Do not be concerned with rejection. Do not be concerned with the sale. The primary focus is to build connections and create friendships.
- People buy from people they know and like.
  - Be likable
  - Be memorable
  - Be visible
  - Be prepared
- People need to know who you are whether they do business with you or not.

Step 7

The Art of Informative Conversation

It's not enough just to identify the client's wants and needs; you have to identify the positive gain they will derive from purchasing your product or service through genuinely interested casual conversation.

1. For example, if a customer wants to buy his wife a piece of jewelry.
2. The jeweler builds a clear understanding of what the customer really wants by narrowing the customer's focus on what he wants to purchase – a ring, for example.
3. Then the jeweler taps into the positive emotional gain of the purchase by asking questions in a casual conversation.
4. In the first questions tap into the positive result of his making the purchase: "How excited do you think your wife will be when she opens this gift?" "How will her response make you feel?"
5. Next identify the negative result of not purchasing – again with casual questions and genuine concern; "When was the last time you surprised your wife with something this amazing?"
6. A good salesman will take the time to really find out what the customer wants and needs – to become the solution to those wants and needs.
7. The jeweler is not selling *his* solution; he's selling *his customer's* solution.

Gain-Pain Conversation Sales

- Don't be so eager to talk about yourself.
- Do the 3-to-1 rule – for every three questions you ask the person, you offer one thing about yourself. Keep your one answer relevant to the conversation.
  - Ask them: What made you choose your profession?
  - What inspired you to be in this industry?
  - What do you like about your career? What is rewarding?
  - What type of sports did you play in high school?
  - What is your favorite movie?
  - What would you recommend as a book that I might find influential and interesting?
- Put yourself in a position of getting (not giving) advice.
- Put yourself in a position of curiosity.
- Put yourself in a position of wanting to understand and learn.
- Through those questions you gain a keen insight into their values and beliefs, the things they don't like, things they do like.
- You do this with prospects, meeting people, dating, and all kinds of personal relationships. There is no difference in doing this in sales.

Step 8

Overcoming Fear of Rejection

The reason sales people fear rejection is because they're selling their own solution and their own vision. When the customer says "no," the sales person's personal vision and solution are being rejected. A different way to approach the sale is to take your ego out of it.

1. Understand the customer's vision first and foremost.
2. Unearth their thoughts about how your solution is going to work for them using the art of casual conversation.
3. Help them understand how the product is going to be a solution for them by letting them try on the product. Do a test drive with questions.
   a. How will it make their life easier?
   b. How will it help their company make more money?
4. Get the customer to utilize the product. That will establish ownership.
5. Show their vision back to them with your product attached.
6. If you do this correctly, you have personally removed yourself from the possibility of rejection. Then, if they say "no," they are rejecting themselves.

Overcoming Fear of Rejection Means Taking Yourself Out of the Problem

- Never put yourself in the position of begging. Put yourself in a position of providing.
- Let the customer paint a canvas of what they want.
- Listen to their vision of the solution.
- They understand their problem – let them tell you their vision of the solution.
- You then have the proper information with which to align your product or service – their vision and solution.
- You then feed their vision and solution back to them incorporating your product.
- At this point, if you did this correctly, they are going to want to give you their business.
- If you didn't do it correctly, ask them more questions. Sometimes they may not have the confidence in themselves to make that decision.
- If they lack confidence they may not be able to make the decision to buy from you because something else may be going on. Sometimes they lack confidence in:
    - Themselves
    - Their resources
    - Their people
    - Their financial situation
- Ultimately, rejection has nothing to do with you.

Step 9

The Power to Give Before You Receive

Earlier I mentioned that you wanted to be your customer's solution. Giving is where that solution begins. If you set your mind to being of service to your customer rather than on making the sale, the sale will come out of that service and will earn you the right to receive their business.

Giving includes:

1. The customer has a problem, a want or a need. Your product, program or service should provide the solution to that problem. It's up to you to have an in-depth understanding of what the customer is looking for in order to show how your product, program or service is his solution.
2. First, understand exactly what your customer wants. Question the customer until you identify her needs and desires.
3. Give your customer the solution to his problem, linked to your product or service.
4. When you have given the customer what she wants in a way that fully serves her, then ask for the business.
5. The essential step is to give something of true value to the client before you can expect to receive his business. This will result in long-term business and referrals as well.

Giving Before You Take Helps Overcome Negative ROIs

- "They've done business with my competition forever."

  Do you think that your competition has taken the time to understand the specific and evolving problems of their client and provided solutions? Or might the level of service have eroded over time?

  A question for a prospective buyer is, "When was the last time you and my competition did a product review?"

- "I'll never reach the decision maker."

  Develop relationships with the key people in the CEO's organization. Use the people in his organization to make your name a buzzword.

  Drop by the corporate office. Introduce yourself to multiple people, including the receptionist. Go to a local pub or nearby eating place where employees gather. Get insights from talking to people.

Step 10

Sell Like a Multi-Billion Dollar Business

What benefits do multi-billion dollar businesses focus on?

They:

1. Make you feel good.
2. Make you look good.
3. Make a delivery that sounds good.
4. Make what you need faster.
5. Make what you do easier.
6. Make what you need more affordable.

Sell your product with those key points in mind.
They tap into the human cravings and emotional aspects
of the five senses.

Multi-Billion Dollar Business

- Feel Good
  - Emotional and physical gratification
    - A widget makes you feel good about yourself.
    - A service gives you peace of mind.
- Look Good
  - Ego Boost
  - Status
  - Self-worth
  - Prestige
- Sound Good (comes from a salesman's belief in the product)
  - A pitch that is appealing to the ear
  - Enthusiastic delivery
- Make it faster
  - Instant gratification
  - Save time
- Make it easier
  - Turn-key, easy to use for self and others
  - Operator friendly
- Make it more affordable
  - The solution will justify the cost

Step 11

Maximize Your Pay Plan

You, as a sales professional, have to have a clear understanding of how you make money.

1. What are the items that give you the greatest commission?
2. What are the items that give you the greatest bonus?
3. What commissionable items sell the most in your marketplace?
4. What additional money-making opportunities will make your employer or the company more money?

When you focus on what benefits you the most you stand out in your company and in your field and you get the lifestyle you want in exchange.

Some opportunities that make your company more money include:

- New products that need to be taken to market.
    - The sales solutions haven't been developed yet, so you become a sales leader.
- Dead inventory.
    - If you focus on things that are not moving that may be costing your company money, ask for an extra bonus for moving that product.
- Reevaluate your day to include where and how to sell the highest commissionable items.

Step 12

The Power of Referrals

One of the biggest things that sales professionals overlook is asking for referrals from people who have already bought. In this case, referral means sending you to people who might become new clients.

1. If they bought from you, that means that they liked you and why wouldn't they refer you to someone else?

2. People pay millions and millions of dollars for lead generation with email lists, phone numbers and software etc. in order to get good testimonials which you can get for free just by doing a good job and taking care of your customers.

3. In order to get a powerful referral you need to do good business. You basically need to be the type of business professional that has garnered so much trust that you would be referred to people's grandparents.

Who to Ask For Referrals

- People to whom you have sold in the past.
- People with whom you have come in contact.
- Friends and family.

How to Get Referrals

- Offer a reward.
- Go into the database of all past clients. Depending on the size of your list, you should target at least ten contacts a day to ask for referrals.
- Even if people you come in contact with are not your clients, if they like you, ask for referrals. The question is, "Who do you know that can benefit from this product, program or service I'm offering?"
- You can't be afraid to ask.You have nothing to lose and everything to gain.
- Take a handful of your best, raving, customer fans and check in with them periodically for potential clients.

Step 13

Setting Daily Money-Making Activities

This should be the highlight of your day. This should be so exciting for you because you are going to create your own paycheck.

1. So many sales professionals go to work aimlessly,instead of examining the potential payment opportunities that are available to optimize. It really is a shame because it affects their:
   a. Paycheck
   b. Results
   c. Lifestyle
2. Failing to set goals leads to having no purpose for each day, month, year and possibly life.
3. Your purpose should be the fuel for your money-making activities. It's not about the money. It's about creating more opportunities for your life.

Setting Daily Challenges

- Make a list of the greatest money-making activities available to you. You are looking for exposures that will give you opportunities for sales.
- You need people to whom to make sales. Create opportunities to meet, contact and connect with people.
- You find those activities by:
    - Making phone calls
    - Sending emails
    - Creating a presence on social media
    - Making in-person cold calls
    - Making follow-up calls
    - Networking
    - Attending classes, seminars and workshops
    - Making appointments
    - Introducing yourself within the various facilities where your potential clients work
- Setting a benchmark for how much money you need for the day and asking yourself what money-making activities you need to do to meet your goals.

Step 14

Appreciate the Business

We need to know, appreciate and respect that customers are not expendable.

1. We need to show appreciation and good customer service for the business we have earned.
2. There are some business entities that abuse and exploit customer service from the salesman. There should be a line.
3. The business relationship should be mutually beneficial, appreciated and fun.
4. Also have an appreciation for the company you represent and the product and service you sell.
5. Appreciation is a 360-degree operation.

Appreciate:
   a. Who you work for
   b. Your customer
   c. Your product or service
   d. Yourself

Appreciate the Business

- Show genuine caring.
- Genuinely listen.
- Be empathetic.
- Be non-judgmental.
- Take responsibility for yourself.
- Go above and beyond the call of duty.
- Be a confidant.
- Most importantly, be a friend.

Step 15

Be a Superstar

What being a Superstar means is being the outstanding person who you, yourself, would want to do business with on every level and in every aspect.

1. Having a life-purpose for yourself and making sure that your product, service or program aligns with that purpose.
2. It is an endless journey of professional development, self-improvement and spiritual enlightenment.
3. Since being a Superstar requires energy, it also includes eating healthy, exercising, getting rest.
4. Boldness, aggression and tenacity are often considered negatives when applied to salespeople. If those qualities are applied to your purpose of solving your customer's problems and giving your customer the best possible service, they become the positives that create super stardom.

Some Important Superstar Qualities

- Be a problem solver.
- Be solution-based oriented.
- Have a powerful, positive attitude.
- Read every sales book. Take every sales seminar that you can. Be a sponge for learning.
- Sharpen your selling skills daily.
- Capitalize on your strengths in the selling process.
- Be relentless.
- Have a thick skin.
- Don't be afraid to ask.
- Don't be afraid of the word "No."
- Be well groomed:
  - Pressed shirt,
  - Hair clean and neat,
  - Shoes polished,
  - Physically appealing to the eye,
  - Have a winning smile.
- Love people.
- Take time to pray.
- Take time to meditate.
- Center yourself for who you really are and how you want to show up in the world.
- Always aspire to have fun.

You've finished. Before you go...

Tweet/share that you finished this book.

Please star rate this book on Amazon.

Reviews are solid gold to writers. Please take a few minutes to give us some itty bitty feedback on this book.

ABOUT THE AUTHOR

Anthony Camacho attributes his selling success to his love of people. He has invested tens of thousands of dollars in books, workshops and seminars to understand human behavior, leadership and influence in order to best serve his clients.

Camacho has in-person cold called millions of dollars in sales through his skill-set of making friends and connecting with people. He was known in his former company as "The Hitman" for his high-closing, new accounts ratio. Now he spends 100% of his time teaching sales professionals, entrepreneurs and multi-million dollar companies how to do the same.

In 2013, at the top of his selling career, he opened his own business as a motivational speaker and sales trainer. His goal is to change the world view of salesmanship both inside and outside of the sales industry.

To expand what you have learned in this Itty Bitty Book, you can attend his live events, request a workshop, and visit his website at:

http://www.topproducerfactory.com

"I would like to thank my grandfather Grandpa Tony Martinez for teaching me the value of a strong work ethic, my grandmother Grandma Dora Martinez for being my first motivational speaker, my beautiful Avatar Princess Wife Candice and my three beautiful princesses Allasondra, Anastasia and Athena for completing my purpose."

Itty Bitty™ Books

The Amazing Itty Bitty Travel Planning Book: *15 Simple Steps to Keep Stress Out of Your Travel Plans* – Rosemary Workman

The Amazing Itty Bitty Weight Loss Book: *15 Simple Steps to Weight Loss Success* – Suzy Prudden and Joan Meijer-Hirschland

The Amazing Itty Bitty Food and Exercise Journal: *Companion to the Itty Bitty Weight Loss Book* – Suzy Prudden and Joan Meijer-Hirschland

The Amazing Itty Bitty Cruise Journal – Itty Bitty Books

...and many more

Also by Anthony Camacho and Coming Soon…

The Million Dollar Cigar – Anthony Camacho

The Enlightened Salesman – Anthony Camacho

The Amazing Itty Bitty Black Book of Sales: *15 Steps to Utilizing Visualization and Creating a Professional Sales Person's Mindset* – Anthony Camacho

The Amazing Itty Bitty Black Book of Sales: *15 Steps to Eliminate Self-Sabotage* – Anthony Camacho

The Amazing Itty Bitty Black Book of Sales: *15 Steps to Unlock the Secrets of In-Person Cold Calling* –Anthony Camacho

The Amazing Itty Bitty Black Book of Sales: *15 Steps that Unlock the Power of Giving Before You Receive*
– Anthony Camacho

The Amazing Itty Bitty Black Book of Sales:*15 Simple Secrets of Setting Daily Money Making Activities*
– Anthony Camacho

Get your FREE gift from Itty Bitty Books
"Create Your Perfect Day"
Delivered directly to your phone
Text 55678 – Code ITTYBITTY in the message place.

www.ingramcontent.com/pod-product-compliance
Lightning Source LLC
Chambersburg PA
CBHW071422200326
41520CB00014B/3528